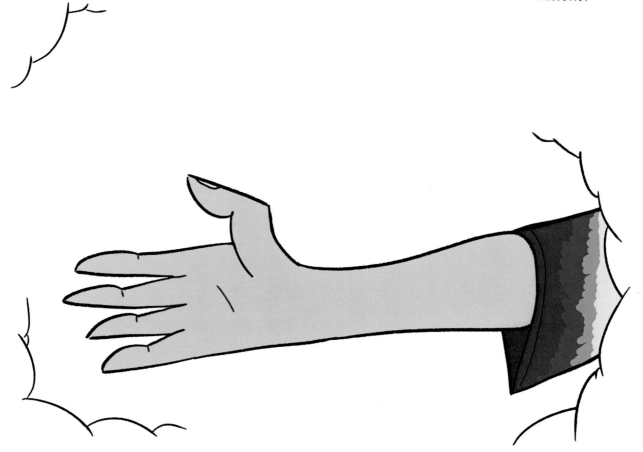

Written By Melissa Buchanan
and Illustrated by Matthew Rose
Inspired by the life and antics of Dan Burress

Let me Tell you About My Grandad

By Melissa Buchanan and Matthew Rose

Guess what, my grandad
is the greatest grandad ever!

My grandad is awesome!
He likes to drive fast!
He enjoys the ride
and doesn't mind the forecast!

My grandad is spectacular!
The stories I could share!
He can fix almost anything and does it with flair!
Often, he also teaches ME how to repair!

My grandad is amazing!
He's always baking something sweet!
Cooking something delicious!
Busy creating something
for us all to enjoy and eat!

About my Grandad...I've just begun!
He learned science and chemistry for fun!
He enjoys scaring us, and teaching us too
Making us laugh, run, and scream!
Boo!

My Grandad is so much fun!
He enjoys going to the Lake!
Boating and fishing and swimming
all his grandkids he will take!

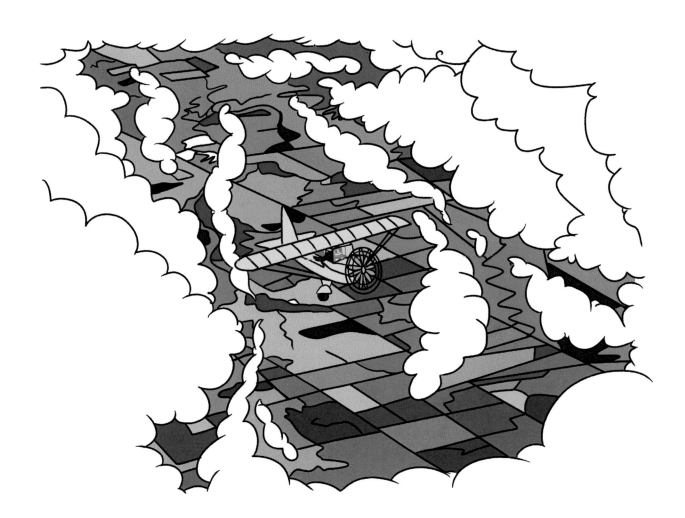

My Grandad is Super!
There is nothing he won't try!
He has so many hobbies, and even
knows how to fly!

My Grandad is Terrific!
Just wait and you'll see!
He makes fireworks that explode
bigger than than the trees!

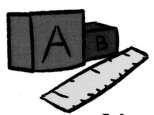

My Grandad Is Wonderful,
In every possible way!
You'll see, he's super cool!
He's coming to pick me up today!

The End

I love you this much

This book is inspired by my
amazing grandfather
Dan Burress, an amazing man
who inspires everyone
in his life daily.
We love you thiiiiiis
much grandad!

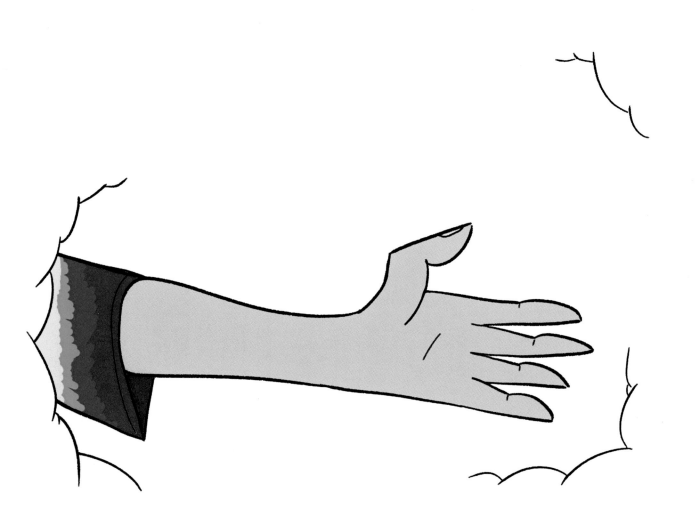

Made in the USA
Coppell, TX
05 December 2024

41808789R00017